A LETTER
TO GREAT BRITAIN
FROM
SWITZERLAND

GENERAL PREFACE

THIS series of books is designed to assist thought upon the relation of the Christian faith to present problems. We live in a changing society; it is still an open question what the outcome of change will be. It is the duty of Christians to be aware of what is happening and, while the situation is still fluid, to exercise their utmost influence upon the course of events. In politics the old party lines are vanishing, and new groups are being formed. Christians ought to play a decided part both by thought and action in these developments. Those who are collaborating in the " Christian News-Letter " and who are producing these books invite all men of goodwill to join with them in an attempt to understand the principles at stake and the policies which must be pursued.

We have got as a nation to do much more hard thinking than has been our wont. It has been said that " the average Englishman not only has no ideas, he hates an idea when he meets one ". During the last hundred years our general security and the settled framework of our society have made thought about fundamental principles to seem unnecessary; but now that change is upon us we must ask the big and difficult questions that have been neglected. There is no law of nature which prevents Englishmen from doing this. We shall, however, find it hard work, and the general reader, for whom these books are intended, must not expect to be let off lightly. This sustained effort of thought, in which it is hoped individuals and groups in every rank of society will co-operate, is likely to unmask truths which we should prefer to ignore and duties which we should prefer not to have to undertake.

A LETTER
TO GREAT BRITAIN
FROM
SWITZERLAND

BY

KARL BARTH

Wipf & Stock
PUBLISHERS
Eugene, Oregon

Wipf and Stock Publishers
199 W 8th Ave, Suite 3
Eugene, OR 97401

A Letter to Great Britain from Switzerland
By Barth, Karl
Copyright©1941 SPCK
ISBN: 1-59244-586-1
Publication date 9/17/2004
Previously published by The Sheldon Press, 1941

CONTENTS

INTRODUCTION

By A. R. Vidler

Professor Karl Barth is probably the most widely known of all living theologians. His name is known to thousands who have never read any of his writings. The adjective " Barthian " has been invented to describe the theological position for which he stands, but, like many such adjectives, it has been much abused, and doctrines to which Professor Barth himself would certainly not subscribe have been carelessly attached to his name. It is to be feared that in England this guilty carelessness has been very common. In particular, " Barthianism " has been used as a synonym for " transcendentalism ", *i.e.*, the doctrine that the Christian Gospel and the Christian Church have to do only with the transcendent, heavenly, other world and that they have no message for, and no dealings with, the affairs of this world. The present letter will at least correct that error. It will not only help us to a more accurate understanding of Professor Barth's own teaching, but also—what, he would agree, is much more important—it will drive us to clearer and deeper thinking about the great theological questions which the war is pressing upon us.

Readers may be glad to be acquainted with the

following facts about Professor Barth. He was born at Basle in 1886, the son of a theological professor at the University of Bern. He studied theology at the Universities of Bern, Berlin and Marburg. At Berlin, Barth, who subsequently became the most redoubtable corrector of " liberal " theology, was a pupil of the famous " liberal " theologian, Adolf Harnack (1851–1930). In 1909 he was ordained at Geneva and was the assistant curate of Adolf Keller, Pastor of the German (*i.e.*, German-speaking Swiss) Reformed Congregation. From 1911 to 1921 he was Pastor of Safenwil (Switzerland). Then he held professorships of theology at Göttingen (1921–25), at Münster in Westphalia (1925–30), and at Bonn (1930–35). It was during the latter period that the German Church conflict came to a head, and in 1935 he was dismissed because of his refusal to take an oath of allegiance to Adolf Hitler which was demanded of him as a State official.[1] Immediately afterwards he was appointed Professor of Systematic Theology at the University of Basle, which is the position he still occupies. Professor Barth has visited this country more than once. In 1937–8 he delivered the Gifford Lectures at Aberdeen. He is a Doctor of the Universities of Aberdeen, Oxford and St Andrew's. Several of his books have been translated into English, and a list of these will be found in the Appendix (p. 53).

In the Appendix there will also be found translations of two letters which Professor Barth wrote to the French Protestants in December, 1939, and October, 1940. These have hitherto been published only in

---

[1] In Germany university professors are State officials.

periodicals. It is fitting that they should be made available in more durable form, and they will be found to throw fuller light on some matters to which only brief allusions are made in the present letter to the Christians of Great Britain.

It will be noticed that in this letter Professor Barth seems to write as though " Natural Law " were a doctrine which is familiar in this country and as though our theologians and others set much store by it. This calls for a word of comment. For " Natural Law " is not a term about which in the modern period we have heard very much from our native theologians or preachers or writers; when we do come across references to it, *e.g.* in Papal Encyclicals, it strikes most of us as unfamiliar and obscure. I am sure, however, that Professor Barth is quite justified in supposing that most British Christians do base their attitude to the war on what is equivalent to a doctrine of " Natural Law ", even though we do not make use of that term and have not sufficiently considered what such a doctrine implies. That is to say, his controversy with us is a real, and not an imaginary one.

Doctrines of " Natural Law " have played an important part in traditional Christian theology,[1] as well as in secular systems of thought,[2] and I should myself say that, whatever is to be our judgment of their truth or authority, we could do with a fuller and more definite exposition of the ideas underlying them than

---

[1] See R. W. and A. J. Carlyle, *A History of Medieval Political Theory in the West,* and Ernst Troeltsch, *The Social Teaching of the Christian Churches.*

[2] See Gierke's *Natural Law and the Theory of Society,* Eng. trans. by Ernest Barker.

is at present available. A similar term, " the Moral Law ", is more familiar to us, though that too needs a good deal more elucidation than is commonly given to it.

Readers of the letter will be near the mark if they understand " Natural Law " to mean that group of ideas which Professor Barth enumerates on page 16, viz. " Western civilization ", " the liberty of the individual ", " freedom of knowledge ", " the infinite value of the human personality ", " the brotherhood of men ", " social justice ", etc. He is in effect asking us whether we realize what we are talking about, and whether we mean what we say.

For the translation of this letter from German into English we are indebted to the Rev. E. H. Gordon, assistant curate of Christ Church, Battersea, formerly a Pastor in the German Confessional Church, and the Rev. George Hill, assistant curate of St. Saviour's Church, Battersea Park.

At Professor Barth's special request all the royalties due to the author will be given to the British Red Cross Society.

A LETTER TO GREAT BRITAIN FROM SWITZERLAND

Dear Christian Brethren in Great Britain,

I have been kindly invited by the Rev. A. R. Vidler and Dr J. H. Oldham to write you a letter in which I may tell you what is in my mind about those things which at the present time stir all of us. They both think that in this way I may be able to do something towards maintaining the link between the Christians of the Anglo-Saxon World and those on the Continent.

I accepted this invitation immediately, but I have been hesitating for a long time to comply with it. Now that I am about to do so, at the outset I want you to believe me when I say that without such an invitation I should hardly have dared thus to address you. I am by no means an Apostle; and, even if I were, after all I have heard and read about you in these last few years, I should feel inclined to say to you with the Apostle Paul: " I myself also am persuaded of you, my brethren, that ye yourselves are full of goodness, filled with all knowledge, able also to admonish one another " (Rom. xv. 14). My main reason for accepting the invitation to write to you is that I want to express what I have been feeling as I have shared with you the anxieties, hardships, tasks and hopes with which you are occupied, and to assure you that I shall continue to share with you in all that lies ahead. But more than that: I want to make it clear that I consider the great cause which to-day lays hold of you to be in a special sense my own cause and the cause of the whole Church and of Christendom. For this reason I do not think that it is the interference of a stranger with your affairs if I tell you briefly my own personal thoughts on this subject. Kindly forbearance on your part will obviously be necessary. I am very eager to find the right door and to discover the right bell on that door: but that is anything but easy. For many years it has been my deep desire to gain a fuller understanding of the general life of your people and country, and especially of your Christian life: I have also studied with interest a good many specimens of your war-time political and theological literature. But I still do not find it easy to see exactly where you stand and to find the right message to send. And this is all the more difficult because the situation is now changing from month to month; and it may easily happen that to-morrow you will no longer be in the situation in which I had, perhaps rightly, thought you to be to-day. May I ask you very kindly to take all this into account, and to forgive me if I should show some misunderstanding of you in the course of what I write; and will you also forgive me if I should not succeed in making myself altogether clear? Should this happen, remember the sincere brotherliness of my intentions!

I have been invited as a Christian and by Christians to write this letter, and it is Eastertide as I put my hand to the task. Together, therefore, we hear the word of Jesus Christ: " All power is given unto Me in heaven and in earth." The fact that this word is true, and that in our own times it will remain and will prove itself true, brings us all and binds us all together. This it is which stirs you over there and stirs me here more deeply than anything else; this it is which lays hold of us more strongly than anything else; this it is which controls us more definitely than anything else. Taking our stand on the truth of this word, you and I look at the events and personalities of our time, and desire, in the face of these events and personalities, to take due account of our responsibilities. Because this word is true, you desire, in the midst of the storm and tumult of this war, to be and to remain good Britons, and you will do so; likewise, I desire to be and to remain a good Swiss, and with God's help I will do so. Everything which to-day we are together seeking to defend, though it may be in different places and in different ways, stands or falls with the truth of this word. I believe that, just because of the truth of this word and in spite of all human limitations, it will not be in vain if I speak my mind to you quite frankly, and if you of your charity will hear with an open mind what I have to say.

Let me begin with an assertion in which I think most of you will find yourselves substantially in agreement with me: we Christians in all lands find ourselves, as far as this war is concerned, in a situation strikingly different from anything that we experienced twenty-five years ago: that is to say, different in so far as we do not just accept this war as a necessary evil, but that we approve it as a righteous war, which God does not simply allow, but which He commands us to wage. And we hold this to be so in spite of the fact that it is not less terrible, and indeed may be much more terrible, than the last war!—in spite of the fact that we believe we have studied the Holy Scriptures since the last war not more superficially but more thoroughly!—in spite of the fact that we think that since the last war we have given deeper consideration to the Christian obligations to the world!—in spite of the fact that since the last war our expectation of the coming of the Kingdom of God and its peace has grown not more feeble but more fervent! In spite of all this, we cannot resist the necessity of giving a different answer to what is to-day a different question. We do not exclude the possibility that the well-known arguments of Christian pacifism, which twenty-five years ago we either made our own or which at any rate deeply disturbed us, may later, in a different situation and in a different form, once again bring us under their power. But on the other hand we cannot deny that at present those arguments, in the form in which we know them, have not this power. We long from the bottom of our hearts for conditions which will allow us men to exist and to live *for* one another, without being forced to exist and to live *in conflict with* one another, as we must when engaged in a dreadful war. Therefore we deeply deplore that war must be waged to-day. But we have no reason to say that it ought not to be waged; no reason to hinder those who are responsible for its conduct; no reason to avoid co-operating in its conduct. Rather we have every reason to acknowledge that this war must be waged, and indeed waged with determination and vigour; we have every reason to devote ourselves wholly to it. We hope that this war will end soon; but it must end in such a way that we shall achieve its object—its limited but essential object. We do not want a compromise, but a decision of the question about which this war is being waged.

We must not overlook the fact that this war is being fought for a cause which is worthy to be defended by all the means in our power—even by war; and, further, that this cause could no longer be defended by any other means than by war. Theoretically both governments and peoples could always settle their national, territorial, economic and strategic aspirations and claims by other than military action; and probably most of the wars which in the past have been waged for such reasons were not necessary—the war of 1914–18 included. But the war which was declared in September, 1939, is not being waged about such things, and it could not therefore be avoided. It is this that renders the pacifist argument unrealistic. People have made much of the various mistakes which after the last war—in the peace treaties, and in the following decade —were committed by the then victors, mistakes which have made this new war possible. But we can maintain no more than that these mistakes made this war *possible*. They did not make it *necessary*. They did not bring it about automatically. They were not of the kind that could be corrected only by the sword. Admittedly the victors of 1918 were astonishingly slow to correct them. But we must not overlook the fact that during those years they were equally slow in consolidating the predominant position which they had won in 1918. Was not the fundamental mistake of those years this—that after the labours and sacrifices which the war had demanded of them, the victorious peoples and their governments tended to indulge their desire for as peaceful a slumber as possible, and consequently did not seriously fulfil their international obligations in any direction? But there are no grounds whatsoever for accusing them of striving to bring about another war in order to maintain and perpetuate the results of the mistakes which had been made. On the contrary, this new war was finally declared only after many years of continued hesitation and evasion, in order to check a movement which was alleged to be an attempt to put right the mistakes which had been made in previous years, but which was actually—and still is—a threat ten times worse than all those mistakes put together. This threat (I need not mention Mussolini, who has proved himself to be a mere lackey) was the attempt of Adolf Hitler to force his " New Order " on Central Europe to-day, on the whole of Europe to-morrow, and on the whole world the day after to-morrow. The essence of this " New Order " is the assertion of the sovereignty of the German race and State, which in practice is that of the German " Führer ". Its establishment is to be achieved by the whole might of Germany's military power, which is impelled by the force of a heathenish religion of blood, despotism (*Autorität*) and war. This enterprise was met by toleration and yet more toleration, in a desire to atone (actually in a very unchristian way!) for past mistakes. It was perhaps through blindness to the true nature and power of this enterprise, perhaps in the weakness which came from a bad conscience about the past, perhaps because they realized they had neglected their duty to arm themselves for war in order to save peace, that the victors of 1918 negotiated with Adolf Hitler, as if those negotiations were concerned with questions which one can and ought to discuss for the sake of peace! They let Hitler and his serf in the South grow stronger and stronger unhindered. They sacrificed Abyssinia and free Spain; and more especially they sacrificed Austria and Czechoslovakia, even though in 1919 they had made themselves responsible for their existence. And at long last, in order to put a stop to this enterprise, when Poland was also overrun in the autumn of 1939 they declared and started the war. It is not true that in this war the West wants to subjugate the East, or the " senile " nations the " youthful " nations, or the " haves " the " have-nots ", or the Capitalists the Socialists. The imperialistic–militaristic demon would have acted somewhat differently from the men who were so slow to make up their minds to enter on this war, and only at long last took their decision! No! the question in this war was and is the very simple and practical one:

Is it right or wrong to exalt, or even to admit, " the Revolution of Nihilism " [1] as the ruling principle of conduct—that is, to adopt the mentality, the language, the standards and the methods of a den of thieves or,

[1] For the significance of this, readers may be referred to H. Rauschning's books: *Germany's Revolution of Destruction* and *The Beast from the Abyss*; also to the *Christian News-Letter*, Supplement No. 80. [EDITOR'S NOTE.]

B

worse still, of the jungle—in order to remove some imperfection in the life of Europe, or to make it more perfect? As soon as some people in responsible positions began to realize that, as far as Adolf Hitler was concerned, what we have to do is simply and solely to defend the Right as such against the Wrong—a matter which did not admit of discussion but demanded the taking up of arms—as soon as they realized this, war broke out.

Since this is so, we Christians cannot say "No" nor "Yes *and* No" to this war; we can only say "Yes". We must postpone our objection to war as such to some future date, when it may once again have some reality. We must not evade our responsibility for seeing that this war is waged, and waged ardently. I say "we Christians" advisedly; meaning all those of us who seek to know God's Word and will in all things great and small, and desire to rule our lives accordingly. We should not, indeed, be Christians if we did not take into account the possibility that it may be God's will to punish us and the whole world, for having done so little to defend the Right, by a Nazi victory and the success of Hitler's evil enterprise. But neither should we be Christians if we were not convinced, just because we admit this possibility, that we must not on any account become Hitler's accomplices by assisting, either actively or passively, in the achievement of what he desires and purposes. Whoever to-day is for Hitler, or is not against him, or is even not wholeheartedly against him, deserves to receive by the will of God through "the Revolution of Nihilism" his due reward. That is the very reason why France—and, first of all, unhappy Germany herself—have by God's will fallen a prey to Hitler's movement. But it is not God's will that we should be likewise guilty and worthy of punishment. On the other hand, it is the clear will of God that we should recognize the true nature and power of the movement, in order to combat it with all our strength. The obedience of the Christian to the clear will of God compels him to support this war.

Can we say this with such certainty? We Christians must say it with such certainty for this reason: the world in which we live is the place where Jesus Christ rose from the dead, and the present age is the time of God's long-suffering until the day when the same Jesus Christ shall come again in His glory. It is on the world in which we live, in all the transitoriness of its present existence, with the sins which we commit and the misery they bring, and with the shadow of death cast over it—it is on this world in its entirety (*im Innersten und doch auch im Äussersten*) that God has set His mark, in that He has exalted the name of Jesus above every name, " that in the name of Jesus every knee should bow, of things in heaven and things on earth and things under the earth " (Phil. ii. 10). Since this is true, the world in which we live is not some sinister wilderness where fate or chance holds sway, or where all sorts of " principalities and powers " run riot unrestrained and rage about unchecked. Since this is true, the world has not been given up to the devil or to man that they may make of it some vast " Insanity Fair " according to the whimsical impulses of some

individual or collective spirits of mischief (*Koboldsgeister*).
There is no doubt that such "principalities and powers",
and indeed such mischievous spirits *do* exist, as the Scriptures say and as we are realizing once again to-day.
But at the same time it is written, and we can and must
hold on to it even to-day: that although at present the
glory of the Kingdom of God is held out to us only as a
hope, yet the Kingly Rule of Christ extends not merely
over the Church as the congregation of the faithful but,
regardless of whether men believe or not, over the whole
of the universe in all its heights and depths; and it also
confronts and overrules with sovereign dignity the
principalities and powers and evil spirits of this
world.

It is indeed true that the whole creation groans with
us, because, as the place where Jesus suffered and
died, it has been made subject to vanity. But it is also
true that this same creation is already consecrated
through the resurrection of Jesus Christ, in expectation
of His coming again and of " a new heaven and a new
earth ". For just as Christ, according to the teaching
of the whole of the New Testament, has already borne
away sin and destroyed death, so also has He already
(according to Col. ii. 15) completely disarmed those
" principalities and powers ", and made a spectacle
of them in His own triumph, in order finally to tread
them down under His feet on the day of His coming
again (1 Cor. xv. 15). It is only as shadows without
real substance and power that they can still beset us.
We Christians, of all men, have no right whatsoever to
fear and respect them or to resign ourselves to the fact
that they are spreading throughout the world as though

they know neither bounds nor lord. We should be slighting the resurrection of Jesus Christ and denying His reign on the right hand of the Father, if we forgot that the world in which we live is already consecrated, and if we did not, for Christ's sake, come to grips spiritedly and resolutely with these evil spirits; and at the same time we should have no more peace in the Church, in our worship of God, in our preaching and hearing of His Word, in our own personal Faith, Love and Hope; we should find in these things no more comfort and strength; we should have to stand ashamed before God and His angels and all His creatures.

The enterprise of Adolf Hitler, with all its clatter and fireworks, and all its cunning and dynamic energy, is the enterprise of an evil spirit, which is apparently allowed its freedom for a time in order to test our faith in the resurrection of Jesus Christ, and above all to test our obedience to that faith.

That an enterprise such as this ought to be resisted by political power using military methods is no new theory, devised merely to suit the present situation. It is precisely Christian thought which insists that resistance should be offered, and it is the Christians themselves who must not withhold their support. This implies, again according to the New Testament, that God has instituted for us Christians not only *the Church*, to build us up in Faith, Love and Hope, but also *the political hierarchy, the State* (for us, and also for the rest of the world), to testify to the Kingly Rule of Christ. Paul called the State in the most solemn way a

" Minister of God " (Rom. xiii. 4, 6). He exhorted the Christians most emphatically to fit themselves into its framework and to pray for its good estate " that we may lead a quiet and peaceable life in all godliness and honesty " (1 Tim. ii. 1). The State which thus counterbalances the Church, and to which Christians are thus bound, is obviously a purely earthly institution. It cannot and must not be regarded as a second Church, much less as a beginning of the Kingdom of God (to which the Church itself can only look forward). When the State speaks we must not expect to hear a confession of Christian Faith, nor when the State acts must we expect to see a demonstration or an example of brotherly love. If we expect too much of the State, we shall fail to appreciate the little that there is to be found. The State embraces the life of all men in as much as the life of all is actually and objectively under the sway of Jesus Christ, even in its unredeemed, and therefore dangerous, natural condition, even apart from the Faith, Love and Hope of the Christian. The State is therefore the sign of that consecration which the world has received through the resurrection of Jesus Christ: it is the sign of the patience with which God bears with, protects and upholds the world until the day when He shall make all things new. Therefore the State is a constant reminder that the self-will of men, the imaginations and confusions arising from their self-conceit, the lusts which they may satisfy as they desire, are not without limits, and that these demons have indeed a master. For, according to Romans xiii. 1–7 and 1 Peter ii. 13–17, the task of the State is this: to discriminate between Right and

Wrong in the lives of all men and to set certain bounds for their conduct. The State must keep constant watch on these bounds, and constantly defend them, first of all *on behalf of* everybody, since the life of all requires such bounds, and then, if necessary, *against* anybody who may be so arrogant as to seek to go round or to break through them. The State was instituted by God to do this, and, as it does this, it is the " Minister of God " in its own sphere and in its own way, just as much as the Church itself. The State bears the sword in order to fulfil this very function. This fact is a solemn judgment on us, but it is God's changeless decree. Where the life of men will *not* be governed by the preaching of the Gospel *nor* by prayer, *nor* by Baptism or the Lord's Supper—in other words, where the bounds of the Church stop—there begins the realm within whose bounds God's fatherly care, which does not fail even there, must be maintained and imposed, if necessary, by the threat of the sword, and, in the last resort, by its use. We have no right to revolt against or to ignore this ordering of human affairs. And indeed, is there any order conceivable other than this so long as human life is not controlled by Faith, Love and Hope? We must be grateful to God that He has not simply given us up to disorder, but that He has given us this order, which is certainly stern but which has proved itself to be effective. Whatever we may say about it, it is an order which sets up a barrier not indeed against sin, but against the chaos into which sin would inevitably plunge us if God had not instituted the State, and if He had not entrusted it with the sword. The State would lose all meaning and would be failing in its duty as an appointed minister of God, and it would be depriving men of the benefits which God, by its function, had intended for them, if it failed to defend the bounds between Right and Wrong by the threat, and by the actual use, of the sword. We Christians cannot desire that the State should be guilty of failing in this duty. We Christians can only pray that it may be a righteous State, in the Biblical sense, whatever the circumstances and whatever the consequences, and we must wholeheartedly work to this end.

When the British Government declared war on Adolf Hitler's Germany in the autumn of 1939, it acted as the Government of a righteous State according to Christian standards. And I believe this was true also of Switzerland when she resolved, at the same time, on the armed defence of her neutrality, the maintenance of which is her historic mission. Since this is so, there is but one decision left to the Christians of your country and of mine, and our Christian obedience compels us to make this decision. The cause which is at stake in this war is our own cause, and we Christians first and foremost must make our own the anxieties, the hardships and the hopes which this war demands of all men. The Christians who do not realize that they must take part unreservedly in this war must have slept over their Bibles as well as over their newspapers.

May I now put a few questions to you, which arose in my mind as I heard the various pronouncements which reached me from your country? It is quite clear to me that we are for all practical purposes united in the attitude towards this war which we as Christians have to take up. But it is not so clear to me whether and how far we are agreed on the foundations for our attitude. Yet it seems to me to be an essential condition of unity between us Christians to-day, not merely that we desire the same things, but that we agree on the reason for our desires. Without this agreement it may easily happen that we shall find ourselves to be at variance even about what we desire. Am I mistaken in assuming that not a few of you have read with some astonishment the brief sketch which I have given you of the reasons for our common resolve? Well, I on my part feel the same when I read some of the reasons put forward by British people for their resolve. My questions are concerned precisely with these reasons, and they may throw some light on what I have been trying to say. Will you please consider these questions in the spirit in which I ask them—namely, as the expression of my sincere desire to be as fully united with you as is necessary in these days?

My main question, which embraces everything else, is concerned with the point from which we Christians must have started in order to arrive at our present decision. The answer to this question will determine whether this decision is Christian or not, and whether we shall remain united in our loyalty to it. You may have been struck by the fact that the ultimate reason which I put forward for the necessity of resisting Hitler was simply the resurrection of Jesus Christ. But I have been struck, on my side, by the fact that in your pronouncements various other conceptions have been put forward as primary and ultimate reasons—such as " Western civilization ", " the liberty of the individual ", " freedom of knowledge ", " the infinite value of the human personality ", " the brotherhood of men ", " social justice ", etc. Now, my question is this: are our intentions really identical, even though the ultimate reasons for them are described in terms which differ so widely from each other? How happy I should be if that were so! There is no need for me to assure you that the terms you use have a very positive meaning for me also, and when I compare them with the terms which are so characteristic of the language of the Third Reich (*e.g.*, *Volk, Rasse, Soldatentum, Lebensraum*, etc.), I do not hesitate for one moment in making my choice between the two: I side wholeheartedly with you. And I would not prevent anybody from speaking constantly of those conceptions with all earnestness and gravity: I do it myself, without being too careful to protect myself against the possibility of being misunderstood. But I doubt whether I can admit that those conceptions do really describe the grounds upon which we Christians must decide on our Christian attitude to the war. That is to say, I am disturbed by the fact that these conceptions are concerned with principles which might also be those of a pious Hindu, Buddhist or Atheist; and that, however beautiful and fruitful they may be, they do not touch at all on the peculiarly Christian truths on which the Church is founded. Do those conceptions sufficiently indicate the distance between us and Hitler? Must we not make the gulf much wider? Ought not our opposition to him to be genuinely Christian? Forgive me if I seem to you to be splitting hairs. But, as some of you know, I took part in the first years of the Church conflict in Germany, which unfortunately has now almost come to a stop, and I learnt there that it is impossible to make any impression on the evil genius of the new Germany by seeking to refute it on the ground of Natural Law, by confronting its evil and dionysian doctrine of man and society with a humane and apollinistic one. The great majority of those (especially of the intellectual emigrants) who have written and spoken against the Third Reich did not understand this. But I would that you, my dear Christian brethren in Great Britain, should understand it: our resistance to Hitler will be built on a really sure foundation only when we resist him unequivocally in the name of peculiarly Christian truth, unequivocally in the name of Jesus Christ. There is admittedly a good Christian interpretation of the ideologies of the eighteenth and nineteenth centuries, and it goes without saying that it is only in their Christian sense that you esteem them so highly. But do not forget that even these ideologies can be interpreted in a pagan sense and thence, by a very short cut, in a Hitlerian sense; and do not forget that clever heads in Germany have long ago done that, and we may well ask where they have been interpreted more skilfully and more forcefully. All arguments based on Natural Law are Janus-headed. They do not lead to the light of clear decisions, but to the misty twilight in which all cats become grey. They lead to—Munich. Everything depends on our having an unambiguous reason for our opposition to Hitler, a reason which makes it impossible to land again in Munich. This reason can derive only from the Ecumenical Creed, as we sought to show at the Synod of Barmen in 1934:

> "Jesus Christ, according to the witness which the Holy Scriptures bear to Him, is the only Word of God, whom we must hear, trust and obey in life and in death. We condemn the false doctrine that the Church can and should recognize as a revelation of God, and so as a source of her preaching, any other Events, Powers, Personalities or Truths beyond and beside this One Word of God."

In the years that followed I endeavoured more than once to find in England and Scotland some understanding of, and agreement with, this declaration. People listened to me with interest, and then gave me to understand that in your country there was no particular need to worry about such theological details. How would even the Oxford World Conference of the Churches in 1937 have reacted to the suggestion that it should so much as consider identifying itself with the German Confessional Church in this declaration? What would I give if the situation were changed to-day! But what really matters is not this declaration as such, but rather the question: Jesus Christ or Natural Law? Is it still too soon to urge on you more earnestly to-day than ever before that Christian decisions as weighty and firm and lasting as they must be in this present crisis can be made only in the name of Jesus Christ, and not in the name of any human ideal? This does not concern some theological fancy which you can put aside by pleading the characteristic Christian tradition of your country; what is at stake is the atmosphere in which alone the Church can live, and in which alone she can speak to the sorely tried people of our time. What is at stake is the preservation or rediscovery of that power which alone will prove a match for the demon of Hitlerism, and which will vanquish it as thoroughly as it must be vanquished if our hopes are to come true. If you can, listen to me now as I plead this cause. And if I am too emphatic—I know that in your country you do not like people to be too emphatic—forgive me! No! we have no time to fight over words. But allow me to put before you some practical consequences which are important for our time, and which arise out of this fundamental truth, in which I desire to be wholly united with you.

If the reason which leads us to our present decision is indeed Jesus Christ, then it will be manifest that this decision is so binding that we have no line by which we can retreat from our obligations. For we know that we Christians are not aliens in the political sphere in which we have taken these obligations upon ourselves; we cannot therefore simply escape from it, leaving it to its own rules and chances. And Jesus Christ does not dwell in some mystic, ritualistic, pietistic, individual-ethical or theological hinterland beyond the political sphere, so that life in real fellowship with Christ begins only outside its bounds. We do indeed rejoice that in the Church we know, worship and proclaim Him, and that, born again through Baptism in His name and nourished and strengthened by His Body and Blood in the Holy Communion, we can live and grow as members of His Body. But because His Rule is not confined within the walls of the Church, and because the political sphere is His, and does not belong to Man or to the Devil, we are irrevocably bound, precisely because we are members of His Church, to serve God in this sphere also. I wonder whether every argument for our political obligations, which is based on Natural Law, does not inevitably lead to a division between the political and Christian spheres; and whether this kind of argument will make our political decision as irrevocable as is necessary if we are to resist the strong temptations which the war brings in its wake.

There is another practical consequence. If the reason for our present decision is indeed Jesus Christ, then that decision will manifest itself in our freedom from all false enthusiasm. I have already called the Righteous State, for whose maintenance against anarchy this war is being waged, a purely earthly institution. And it will become clear that this is so, if we place ourselves for Jesus' sake at the service of this State. And it will then also become clear to us that it cannot be our job to fight God's battle against His enemies, since that battle has already been fought and won on the cross of Golgotha. And further: it will become clear to us that it is not up to us to defend or to extend the Kingdom of God by this war, since the Kingdom will come of itself in Jesus Christ, when His hour comes, without our assistance, political or otherwise. We shall not regard this war, therefore, either as a crusade or as a war of religion. We shall spare ourselves the peculiar passions and the vain expectations and hopes which are wont to be bound up with such an undertaking; we may safely leave all such things to the modern Mohammed and his deceived hordes. What, then, is this war? It is a large-scale police measure which has become absolutely necessary in order to repulse an active anarchism which has become a principle. It seems to me to be theologically significant that it is in this spirit that the British statesmen—I remember the characteristic pamphlet of Harold Nicolson, *Why Britain is at War*—have decided on it and waged it from the very beginning. And it seems to me that Christians also would do well to regard it in the same way, and only in that way. This is the only kind of war which we may be commanded to wage. Any other kind would be an encroachment on the sovereign rights of God, and we Christians should be the last to be guilty of that. Nor should we then have the great calm which is necessary for this hard task. I am afraid that if we stay ourselves on Natural Law rather than on Jesus Christ, we shall not be able to avoid political fanaticism, or to distinguish between our service of God in the Church and in the State, or between our Faith in the coming of God's Kingdom and the simple works which spring from that Faith. I fear the confusions and disappointments which will inevitably follow. We need clear heads more than ever to-day.

There is a further practical consequence. If the ground for our present decision is indeed Jesus Christ, then it will be made manifest by our acting on His precept, " Be not anxious for to-morrow." That is to say, we are not bound by any definite conceptions, expectations and promises with regard to the peace which will follow this war. It is not necessary for us or others to busy ourselves about plans and pictures of the economic and social, national and international, and lastly the religious conditions in the new order which must be established after this war. We shall not set our hearts on such " peace aims ". There is no reason why we should not dream about such " peace aims " as occasion offers. But we shall always remember that we cannot do more than dream about these things. We shall guard against founding our willingness, and the willingness of others, to do our best to-day on such definite expectations and promises. Why? Because if we are serving Jesus Christ we shall know that the ordering of what will be salutary and necessary *after* we have obeyed Him to-day will be *His* concern, and that *then* He will certainly not fail to set us to work on new tasks in His service. It cannot be the concern of good servants, as they obey their Lord's command for to-day, to be continually worrying about what they think He might or should entrust to them and command them to do to-morrow, after they have been obedient in His service to-day. Are they not fully occupied with what is demanded of them to-day? Are they not fully assured by the knowledge that they are to-day serving Him, and have therefore the shelter of His protection and His promises? *Must* they know what will be the outcome of their work, or what they will have to do on the morrow? Is it not a distinct blessing that in fact they cannot know these things at all?

The British Government has as yet refrained—and, as I think, very wisely refrained—from competing with

Hitler's fantastic visions of a New Order in Europe and in the world by publishing any peace aims of its own. At the same time it was probably wise of the Government to allow the British public to discuss openly such peace aims, as has been recently announced. But I believe that British Christians should follow the example of their Government and take as little advantage of this permission as possible; and that they should not add to the number of fantastic plans for the future which are current to-day, by painting all sorts of Christian pictures of this kind, for instance, that of a great Christian World Conference under the presidency of the Roman Pope. Have we still not observed the simple fact that we cannot shape the future in the smallest things, not to speak of the great? Have we still not observed that the only thing that the future demands of us is that we should be ready for it? And that our readiness for the future is complete only when we submit to the demands of the present, and when we accept the assurance which even in the present is not denied to us. Should we not lay hold of the strong confidence that, if this war is waged well so that it achieves its aim, it will definitely be followed, like every piece of work well done, by a new piece of work, which must then be begun—in this case, the work of building the peace when the time comes, even though at the moment we cannot visualize its character and bent? If we base our arguments on Natural Law rather than on Jesus Christ, then I do not know how we shall be able to lay hold of that confidence. If men either openly or secretly consider Natural Law to be the revelation which governs their attitude, then they can-

c

not help escaping from the present and taking refuge in some self-made shape of things to come. Those who do not seek to escape from the present, because they were guided into it by Jesus Christ, need no such refuge.

And here is one other practical consequence. If Jesus Christ is indeed the reason for our present decision, then it will be made manifest in the humility and sincerity of the faith in which we do what we have decided.

First, in *humility*. It is evident that the continued existence in the world of some form of political order (however imperfect and however needful of reformation it may appear) is not due to human worth, but rather to the working of God's grace and patience; and it is only by His grace and patience that we have the honour of co-operating in its protection and defence. Chaos might long ago have swallowed it up. It is extraordinary with what indifference, as if they were mere spectators, even sometimes with what secret sympathy, people in all lands looked on, as this chaos grew greater and mightier in Germany, and as later it began to overrun the borders of Germany. How the masses rejoiced, and how the church bells rang to summon people to thanksgiving services, when Mr Chamberlain and M. Daladier returned from Munich, as if what happened there had been a great salvation! How the few who, in those years, raised their voices to give warning, were ignored and even suspected! How many victims had to be offered up before at long last we woke up, and at long last began to be thankful for the divine mercy which gave us the body politic! We cannot forget all this to-day. Since those days we have certainly not become wholly different beings; and, if we were left to ourselves, we should not be absolutely secure from the possibility of being guilty again of a similar complacency in a different situation. If God did not Himself protect and defend His own cause in this world, we assuredly should do it very badly. We have every reason to glorify Him that—in spite of all this—He has called us to serve His cause and that He will use us therein. We must remember all this when we think of the poor Germans, against whom we must fight to-day even though we have shared their guilt long enough. They were exposed to stronger temptations and cleverer deceptions than we. We stand with them before God, even while of necessity we withstand them to-day with the utmost determination. We are defending ourselves against their own or their Hitler's pride. We shall be able to do it effectively only if we do it in great humility.

And, secondly, in *sincerity*. Faith is sincere when—heeding as little as possible the whisperings of human optimism—it is directed wholly towards God and the victorious power of His will. It is certainly right and necessary to assemble and to put in action all our forces in order to master the tasks which to-day are pressing on us. But it will not do to rely on ourselves, or our aircraft, or our tanks, or our " inexhaustible resources ", or our shrewdness and our morale. It will not do to deny that the devil has even more self-confidence, and that he is probably even richer in all these material and spiritual possessions than we are. Only one thing will do, namely, to put our whole confidence in God alone, so that in this exclusive confidence we may do any and everything which it is in our power to do. This one thing alone will do, because only when we have put our whole confidence in God shall we face, with wide open— not pessimistic but undeceived—eyes, the difficulties and obstructions which we have to overcome, and meet them accordingly.

As I look back on the past eighteen months of war, this question comes insistently into my mind: have we not more than once regarded the situation with a pretty self-confidence, only to be forced to discover afterwards that the devil was always a bit cleverer, quicker and stronger than we had imagined? And further, would it not be more practical to let sincere faith, which brings all our self-confidence to rest in confidence in God, have the first word when we assess the situation at any given time?

We need in our time precisely such a humble and sincere faith in order to resist Hitler. But I ask your pardon, my dear British friends, if I here again point out that, as far as I can see, there is in Natural Law no basis for this faith. Only faith in Jesus Christ can be such humble and sincere faith.

———————

May I ask you once again to take all that has been said as questions to which I do not expect an answer, but by which I want to show you the points on which I should like greater assurance of our common agreement? But now let us have done with questions. If I were not a Doctor of three British universities, I could not claim even the formal right to have this little disputation with you in spirit. But you may at any rate rest assured of this: I have been told, and I have myself eventually been convinced, that the real life of the British Churches and Christians appears only in part, and in smaller part, in the style and accuracy of their Christian and theological language, which we on the Continent think so important. I often think especially about the thesis that the Anglican Communion desires to be understood not from its doctrine, but only from its *worship*, that is, to be exact, only from personal participation in its daily worship. I am therefore fully prepared to admit that the actual agreement between you and me may be far deeper than I have suggested by putting so many questions to you in continental fashion.

Allow me now to end with two observations of a completely different kind.

1. I should like you to know how genuinely edified we have been since last August by hearing of the bearing of the population of London and other British cities under the terrible affliction of German air attacks. The news of this has done not a little towards restoring the confidence of many among us, who because of the happenings in France had become rather doubtful. The hundreds of thousands of defenceless men and women of your people who had to take such hard blows during this time and yet always showed so much patience, humour and constancy, so much ability and readiness to help each other, have given us an example which we hope would in a similar situation be followed

by many in this country. We are grateful to these men and women, since we know that their endurance is indirectly a blessing to us.   I have no doubt that the tradition and the present influence of Christianity in Britain have a special share in this magnificent active and passive achievement. And let me whisper in the ear of those of you who know me more closely that, in the face of these events, I am inclined to judge more mildly much of the " pelagianism " [1] with which from time to time I had to reproach my British friends.

2. There is no need for me to hide from you my personal conviction that in the end Great Britain will be successful in the present war. To-day, as I write, the Germans are marching against Mount Olympu , and at the same time against the Pyramids, and who knows whether they may not one day march against Mount Sinai, too? I cannot therefore venture to prophesy when, where and how Great Britain will conquer. But that she will conquer I am sure, because I have ultimately more confidence in British toughness than in German energy, and because ultimately I ascribe greater historical weight to the better cause, for which the British Empire has made itself responsible, than to the evil and fundamentally fantastic cause of Adolf Hitler. You will understand that all this is humanly speaking, and men make mistakes. But the *faith* in which we decide on our attitude towards this war, is altogether independent of the question who

[1] Pelagius, a British monk of the 4th–5th centuries, denied the orthodox doctrine of original sin and maintained that the human will is of itself capable of good works without the assistance of divine grace. He was fiercely combated by St Augustine. [EDITOR'S NOTE.]

will win. You should know that speaking as a man, and at the risk of making the mistakes of a man, I expect with you that Hitler's dream will have vanished after this war. Napoleon once marched on Moscow. I am certainly prepared for many more nasty surprises and reverses. The way your Mr Churchill is not afraid to warn the public again and again that they may come makes him in my eyes very trustworthy. Perhaps you on your part will remember sympathetically that Switzerland is also an island to-day, surrounded not by mere water, but by the forces of Hitler and Mussolini, and that the German frontier lies only a few miles from Basle. I am, moreover, fully prepared for the menace which threatens us to change completely in character. But the final result of the whole affair I have never doubted, I do not doubt to-day, and I shall not doubt in the future.

But our citizenship, our *politeia*, is to-day and always in heaven. For this very reason, we can and we shall to-day and always be of good cheer and firmly resolved in our attitude towards the earthly political order, which is the burning issue of our time.

I greet you cordially in the fellowship of a common Faith and Purpose.

Yours,
KARL BARTH.

Basle, April 1941.

APPENDIX

I

First Letter to the French Protestants [1]

As you say in your letter, three-quarters of the French theologians whom I had the privilege of meeting and with whom I had the privilege of working in Bièvres in January this year are to-day serving your country in a military capacity at the front or elsewhere. You invite me to send to them and to my other friends in France a message through *Foi et Vie*. I do so with great pleasure, since it gives me the opportunity of telling you what moves me at this present time as I think of you all.

Our situation here in Basle is such that we cannot possibly shut our eyes to the war. Only a few kilometres from here the fortifications begin. On the right are the German fortifications and on the left the French. The pilots of both sides are, I am afraid, in the habit of forgetting that they have no business in the air above our heads. It has even happened that certain undesirable objects have fallen from above upon our territory. In the midst of our streets the barricades and barbed wire of our defences bristle ready to meet an even worse menace. Such are the circumstances in which I have to expound the peaceful mysteries of Christian Dogmatics, just now the Doctrine of Predestination.

But what is that compared with the problems and cares which are your concern to-day—you yourselves, your families, your congregations and the whole Reformed

---

[1] This letter was addressed to a French Pastor, Editor of *Foi et Vie*. The English translation, reproduced here, was published in *Theology*, March, 1940.

Church of your land? You may rest assured that I myself and many others in our still " neutral " part of the world realize what turmoils and hardships, what sacrifices and temptations events have brought and continue to bring to you. We know, too, that we are bound as Christians to share with you and with everyone in the belligerent countries in your anxiety and affliction: and we do this from the bottom of our hearts. You will not, dear friends, misinterpret the fact that we Swiss form at present an island of " neutrality " from a military point of view. At the moment there is no other possibility. The causes of the present war lie in the international decisions of 1919 in which our country did not take part. And since that date (as before) high politics in Europe have developed without our co-operation. Switzerland would become guilty of the same arbitrary methods in politics, the curbing of which is the task of to-day, if she voluntarily disregarded her re-peatedly declared policy and entered the war as a belligerent without the compulsion of external pressure. For the moment we have a duty towards the whole of Europe—the duty of preserving the integrity of that piece of European order which has been entrusted precisely to us in the form of military neutrality. You will agree with me when I say that it is necessary and salutary for all nations, and not least for the Church of Jesus Christ in all nations, that there should be, as long as possible, such places through which it is possible to maintain contact between men and Christians in some sort of tranquillity. Such a place is Switzerland for the time being. "Neutrality", interpreted in this sense, is laid upon us as an obligation for the time being. This neutrality signifies, not that we dissociate ourselves from The Event of our time, but that we associate ourselves with it in our own *particular* way. It signifies the special form of *our* responsibility in Europe. There are probably few Swiss who understand our "neutrality" in any other sense. At any rate I should like it to be known that I personally understand it in this sense and in this sense alone.

There can be no doubt that this war is for all of us, for belligerents and neutrals alike, a very special war, that it bears a totally different character from the war of 1914 and from nearly all the wars of previous centuries. France and England hesitated long (perhaps too long, but when one considers the grim character of this *ultima ratio*, this hesitation was certainly justified) before they took up arms to put an end to the arbitrary use of the law of might (*Faustrecht*) which the present German Government has openly proclaimed and put into practice with ever-increasing unscrupulousness. After having made Germany from end to end a land of fear and terror, Hitler's National Socialism has become to an increasing extent a menace to the whole of Europe. This menace has led to an awakening. In the midst of the sin and shame of all nations there still remains, through the goodness of God, something of law and order, of free humanity, and above all, and as that which gives its meaning to all else, of freedom to proclaim the Gospel. Where Hitler reigns, even this remnant is destroyed. But Hitler is not satisfied to reign in Germany alone. When this last fact became sufficiently clear for even the blind to see, war came. " Il faut en finir ! " said your Prime Minister in the hour of decision, and his English colleague repeated this declaration. The question as to how deep this resolve and this determination go may safely be left to the sense of responsibility of these statesmen. It is certain that every Christian too, who has followed the last years with his eyes and ears opened, must, just because he is a Christian, give his own Yes and Amen to this " Il faut en finir ! " Undoubtedly, France and England have had in the past, and still have, their own imperialistic motives for waging this war. That, however, does not make any difference. Our generation would be answerable before God and before men if the attempt were *not* made to put an end to the menace of Hitler. In the end war remained the only means of achieving this purpose. France and England had to undertake the task, because they are chiefly responsible for the state of affairs which arose in Europe after 1919—because they are responsible, too, for making Hitler possible. But, now that they have undertaken the war, it cannot well be denied that in this war not only the interests of France and England are at stake, but also those of *all other* nations—in the end even the interests of the German nation itself. Herein lies the peculiarity of this war. It has arisen from the mortal jeopardy of all, and it must be waged in the defence of all. We " neutrals ", too, are not neutral in so far as we know full well that the efforts and the sacrifices of this war are necessary to preserve for *us* too what is more indispensable for life than life itself. Our French and English friends, and our German friends as well, should know that we are grateful to those who, in accordance with their historical position and responsibility, have taken upon themselves the waging of this war against Hitler.

The Church of Jesus Christ cannot and will not wage war. She can and will simply pray, believe, hope, love, and proclaim and hearken to the Gospel. She knows that The Event by which we poor men are succoured in an effectual, eternal and godly way has come, comes, and will come to pass, not, according to Zech. iv. 6, by force of arms or by power or by any kind of human effort and achievement, but only by the Spirit of God. The Church therefore will not see in the cause of England and France the *causa Dei*, and she will not preach a crusade against Hitler.

He who died upon the Cross died for Hitler too, and, even more, for all those bewildered men who voluntarily or involuntarily serve under his banner. But precisely because the Church knows about justification which we men cannot attain by any means for ourselves, she cannot remain indifferent. She cannot remain " neutral " in things great or small where justice is at stake, where the attempt is being made to establish a poor feeble human justice against overwhelming, flagrant injustice. Where this is at stake, there the Church cannot withhold her witness. It is the command of God that justice be done on earth: it is precisely for this purpose that God has instituted the State and given to it the sword; and, despite all the shortcomings of which it may otherwise be guilty, the State which endeavours to defend the right proves itself precisely by these endeavours to be a Just State, and may claim the obedience of everyone. It would be regrettable if the Christian Churches, which in previous wars have so often and so thoughtlessly spoken the language of nationalism and of militarism, should just in this war equally thoughtlessly decide to adopt the silence of neutrality and pacifism. The Churches ought to-day to pray in all penitence and sobriety for a *just* peace, and in the same penitence and sobriety to bear witness to all the world that it is necessary and worth while to fight and to suffer for this *just* peace. They certainly ought not to persuade the democratic States that they are, so to say, the Lord's own warriors. But they ought to say to them that we are privileged to be *human* and that we must *defend* ourselves with the power of desperation against the inbreaking of open inhumanity. The Churches owe the duty of witnessing to the Christians in Germany as well as to the whole German nation: Your cause is not just! You are mistaken! Have no more to do with this Hitler! Hands off this war! It is his war alone! Change your course while there is yet time! Why have the representatives and organs of the ecumenical movement preserved so diplomatic a silence in all these years, and even during the fatal developments of this summer and autumn, as if there were no prophetic ministry of Jesus Christ, and as if the Church had no duty of watchfulness? Why have we heard and why do we continue to hear, and that not infrequently, voices of an eschatological defeatism, a defeatism which, appealing to the truth that " the whole world lieth in the evil one ", busies itself almost cynically with asserting that Hitler's present adversaries for their part are no saints either? The apprehension of the truth that God alone is holy will not excuse us from the duty of putting up a resistance to-day. On the contrary, the Church in every land will have to give much comfort in the dark times upon which, according to all appearances, we are entering. The Church, however, will only be able to give real *comfort* if she can also, without hatred or pharisaism or without any illusions concerning the goodness of any human beings, give *admonishment*, if she will earnestly and frankly say that to-day resistance is necessary.

And it will be particularly the Church of Jesus Christ that will at the same time no less clearly recognize and proclaim that other truth, that the ultimate in war—and in this war especially—cannot be war. War is like a painful yet purposeful surgical operation; it can only be waged in order to help, to heal and to secure life. The time may very soon come when there will arise in every country the urgent necessity of bringing this aspect of the matter into the foreground.

My dear French friends, you know how closely I am associated with Germany, with her Church and with her people. You will, I know, not take it amiss, if I ask you both individually and collectively, to concern yourselves even now with the question of what ought to happen if the disaster which Germany has brought upon herself is manifested in her defeat, a defeat which according to all human calculation is inevitable. At the beginning of the war the slogan was announced that the war was not directed against the German people but only against its present rulers. This was a noble formula, but it was an over-simplification of the problem. The new slogan, however, that every people gets the government it deserves, and that the whole German people must be held responsible for the actions of its government, is again too simple. The truth lies somewhere between these two poles. The German people are not wicked as a people, are not at any rate more wicked than any other people. The idea that to-day they must be punished as a whole is an idea which is impossible both from a Christian and from a human point of view. But Hitler's National Socialism is most certainly the wicked expression of the extraordinary political stupidity, confusion and helplessness of the German people.

Let me just sketch the causes and the real significance of this fact as I understand them. The French people and the English people are no more " Christian " as a people than are the Germans. But the German people suffer from the heritage of a paganism that is mystical and that is in consequence unrestrained, unwise and illusory. And it suffers, too, from the heritage of the greatest Christian of Germany, from Martin Luther's error on the relation between Law and Gospel, between the temporal and the spiritual order and power. This error has established, confirmed and idealized the natural paganism of the German people, instead of limiting and restraining it. Every people has just such an heritage from paganism and from certain Christian errors which have strengthened this paganism. Consequently every people has its evil dreams.

Hitlerism is the present evil dream of the German pagan who first became christianized in a Lutheran form. It is a particularly evil kind of dream, a dream which endangers the life both of the Germans themselves and of the rest of us as well. Apart from the torment which it has caused the dreamer himself, this dream has made the dreamer a menace for Europe. He must in the first place be rendered harmless.

It is essential that those who now face the German as an adversary in war and all who may later find themselves face to face with him (if they will themselves think as Christians and not as heathen) should not lose sight of the fact that in this adversary they have to deal with *a sick man*. Particularly when the war is over—and even now we cannot devote too much thought to what must be done when the war is over—it will be necessary to treat him as a sick man is treated. Very firm yet very compassionate hands will then be necessary. Of course, it will be imperative to render physically impossible any further developments on the fatal course which leads from Frederick the Great through Bismarck to Hitler. It will be even more imperative to make manifest to the German people an illustration of that political wisdom which as yet is so foreign to them. By this I mean that there must be created for them *conditions of life* of such a kind that they will be prevented from going on dreaming that evil dream in some new form or other. The illusion that they can only stand their ground against other nations by terrorism must be eradicated from them by an unconditional resolve on the part of these other nations to *do justice* to Germany's real needs as they are conditioned by her geographical situation. That does not mean that Germany should be granted the freedom to become what Bismarck and Hitler wanted to make her. But it does mean that Germany should be granted the freedom to live by her own labour. It cannot be said that this freedom was granted to her in 1919, or in the period from 1919 to 1933. It is for this reason that every nation has its share in the responsibility for the rise of Hitlerism. I myself lived in Germany at the time of the occupation of the Ruhr, and, after that experience, I know what I am saying. It may be that the coming peace will have to be sterner than the peace of Versailles, sterner both politically and militarily. But it will have to be a wiser and a juster peace if all that we have gone through is not to be in vain once more. If this peace is to be wiser and more just it will have above all to show *more care and consideration*. We shall have to allow the population which occupies the wide area of Central Europe and which is set at such a disadvantage through the limitations of the natural re-sources of this area, to share in the means of life which other more fortunately situated nations enjoy. This must be done in such a way as will allow Germany to renounce that fatal course and to bring out her peculiar gifts—there can be no doubt of their wealth and significance—so that she may become to herself and to the other nations a blessing, and not ever and again a curse.

The long entertained desire to give Hitler " a chance " proved dangerous. But it would prove still more dangerous if, after the war, no readiness were shown to give the German nation an honest chance. The mistake of 1919–1933 must not be repeated. The present resistance to the German menace would otherwise be from the very outset without meaning. Otherwise it would be even physically impossible to destroy the German menace by political and military resistance. This is what people in France, too, should clearly realize.

But, my dear friends, I think it would be very unchristian, and therefore very imprudent, if we pondered all these con-siderations without at the end making the frank confession that man proposes—and it is man's duty to propose—but God alone disposes. We can and we should shoulder our responsibilities, our political responsibilities and, if need be, our military responsibilities. But it does not lie with us to determine what will be the eventual issue. And in no circumstances should we have the right to marvel or to complain if the issue were wholly different from the hope and intention, the plan and resolve which we envisage at present. The outcome of this war is not to be predicted with absolute certainty by any calculation of man. I have no need to remind you that Germany is a doughty adversary. You must not think merely of her *capacity for military achievement*, but perhaps still more of the almost unaccountable *capacity for suffering* which the German people possess. This last is one of the best features of their natural and Lutheran heritages. And somewhere behind Germany stand the great enigmas of Russia, and of Italy too, enigmas which may find their solution in this way or that. Even if human calculation gave a hundred per cent. certainty, we as Christians have to remind ourselves that there are such things as " miracles of the antichrist ", absolutely un-expected and astounding achievements of the " beast from the abyss ", which God has His own grounds for permitting, the occurrence of which could for the time being bring to nought all the calculations, not only of the " rational " portion of mankind but also of the Church and of Christians, be these calculations never so well grounded. We do not know whether Hitlerism is not capable of such a miracle— there is much in its development hitherto which tends in this direction. Perhaps a question mark is yet being set over against that admirable resolve, "Il faut en finir ". Perhaps the nations of Europe may be destined to resist this enemy in vain and finally to have to live a life of dishonour under the rule of undisguised Lie, a life com-

D

parable to that of men and Christians in Germany to-day. We are defending ourselves against this menace. We ought not to grumble if this threat were to become an accomplished fact despite all our wishes. We must realize that we shall then receive the due reward of our deeds. The use we all have made of that heavenly gift, that remnant of a free humanity, of democratic justice, and above all of the freedom of the Gospel, has not been such as to oblige God to preserve us from destruction. If we are preserved, it will be only by His grace. Are we prepared to be forced to recognize His grace even perhaps in His *not* preserving us? Are we prepared for a situation in which the defenceless confession of Jesus Christ is the only course left open to us? Are we prepared even then and under such conditions to remain loyal to our God and to rejoice in Him and to find our dignity in this and in this alone? On our answer to this question depends our title to defend ourselves now, depends our right to have a clear conscience in so doing, and our right wholeheartedly to ask God for His assistance. We must be prepared for God, just when we are acting in obedience to His command, to confront us with *His own* " Il faut en finir ", and again by His command to lead us to something *wholly other*. We must be prepared to adhere *to Him* then and especially then, resolved upon a new obedience. Done in this spirit of preparedness, our work of resistance will then be a good work. Then and only then can it be offered with joy and confidence. We are both allowed and obliged to know that God will reign in any case and that He makes no mistakes.

When this letter reaches you, my friends, it will soon be Christmas. Then we, together with the whole of Christendom, which is poor and yet so rich, and with all the angels in heaven, shall be privileged to rejoice in the presence and Kingly Rule of Him who is our salvation and blessedness wholly and in every situation. As the people that walk in darkness, we see a great light. That our duty and privilege is—each in his own place—to watch, to stand fast in the faith, to quit us like men and to be strong—let that be our message to you this Christmas.

KARL BARTH.

December, 1939.

II

SECOND LETTER TO THE FRENCH PROTESTANTS [1]

DEAR FRIENDS AND BRETHREN,

On this occasion it was one of the youngest of the ministers of the Gospel in your country who took upon himself to urge me, as Pastor Westphal did last year, to address you in an open letter. In view of the developments which have taken place in the interval I have for long felt an obligation to follow up in some way what I wrote a year ago.

My last letter had in the main a friendly and understanding reception. I may therefore hope that what I now wish to write to you will not be regarded as the unwarranted interference of an outsider and non-participant.

In the need and task of our time there are no outsiders and non-participants. There may be many who think themselves such, but none are so in reality. This is much plainer to-day than it was a year ago. The war between the nations, which had then begun as a smouldering fire and has since become an all-devouring flame, is the necessary form of a conflict which is not confined by national boundaries, but cuts right across the nations (including the neutrals and not least the Germans themselves), and which everywhere in one way or another compels men to a clear and binding decision—to a Yes or a No, in full view of all conceivable consequences. We all find ourselves immersed n this conflict. We are all involved in its origin and continuance, and we are all, on one side or other of the gulf, nvolved in its solution, whatever this may be, as sharers

---

[1] Reprinted from the *Christian News-Letter*, Supplement No. 66.

in common action, common responsibility, common guilt and common suffering.

These being the grounds on which I take the liberty to address you again, dear fellow-believers in France, I can without further preface explain to you at once what are the question and the request I wish to put to you.

First, the question. It is true, is it not, my French friends, that we are agreed with regard to what has just been said? We were so a year ago. And surely we are so to-day—that is, after, as well as before, all that has happened? It is true, is it not, that the armistice concluded between France and Germany has not altered in any respect the fact that you too are still, and even more now, involved in the conflict which is the root cause of the war, and in the responsibility for the existence of the conflict and for its solution.

And now to add to this question my request. We know how much you are necessarily preoccupied at present with your particular national need and task. But you will not withdraw into it, as though it were your own private concern? You will not seek after solutions which would lead you to a neutral attitude in face of the great decision which now, as before, confronts you, as it does all of us, and on which in the last resort—for you in particular—nothing less than all depends? We count on you that, as Christians and as Frenchmen, you will not leave us in the lurch, but will stand with us on the same side of the abyss—stand with us both inwardly, with your faith and prayers, and—as a result of this—according to your insight and your ability, also outwardly, with your words and deeds, just as definitely as a year ago—nay, more definitely and convincedly, because of the added experience and knowledge of the past year. Just because we love and respect France now as much as before, we cannot and will not, for the sake of any specifically French concern, let you go. We need you.

Do not separate your cause from ours, since ours, as truly now as formerly, is also yours.

I have been told that many of you after the events of last summer have remembered and pondered over the last part of my earlier Christmas letter, where I said that it was unchristian and unwise not to reckon with the possibility of the war taking a turn quite contrary to our wishes and expectations, with " signs and wonders of the Antichrist ", with a coming judgment of God on ourselves, and that we must be ready to submit ourselves to the will and commandment of God even in such unwished-for circumstances. Then and only then, if we were prepared even for that, I wrote at that time, could the necessary work of resistance against Hitler's National Socialism be joyfully and confidently accomplished. That was in no sense an attempt to assume the rôle of a prophet. I wrote as I felt I must write in the circumstances of that time in the discharge of my responsibility to the Holy Scriptures. What actually took place in May and June I, just as little as others, did not at all foresee. It was certainly not a good omen that the French censor then thought it necessary to suppress the last part of my letter as " defeatist ". It may be that the reason why the French resistance could not be so joyful and confident as to become effective was that men were too little ready to take into account that man proposes but God disposes.

However, be that as it may, the very thing happened which we had all least desired and expected, worse than the worst we had imagined. I may tell you that my brother Peter Barth, who died on the evening of June 20th, in the extreme weakness of the last hour of his life exclaimed, " But we will not withdraw beyond the Loire ! "   " We "— do understand, dear French friends, that many of us during those weeks were living in immediate union with you. Yet you (and we with you) had to withdraw far, far beyond the

Loire. I need not here enter into details, which are better known to you than to me, and I for my part have no wish to use any of the harsh words which have been spoken and heard often enough in France itself to describe and explain that whole happening. Whatever the thing may be called, and whatever accusations or self-accusations may be made in regard to it, it was a simple fact that the military capacity of Hitler's Germany was able on this occasion to gain the upper hand, and that after Poland, Norway, Denmark, Holland and Belgium, France too is prevented for the time being from further co-operation in the necessary war against that Germany. It has come to pass that just in these circumstances you have now to submit yourselves to God's will and commandment.

But if, as is probably the case, you are more inclined to-day to remember especially that last part of my Christmas letter, I must also ask you to lay to heart that in the rest of what I then wrote to you there is nothing that needs to be taken back to-day. What change has there been, so far as you are concerned? This, certainly, that to-day for the time being (for the duration of the armistice) you have reasons—I refrain from enquiring whether they are good or bad reasons—for not wanting any longer, or at least not at present, to carry on the war. But there is one thing, surely, that has not changed even for you, but has rather been strengthened; the reason that is to say, which led you a year ago—led you as Christians—to endorse this very same war and to prosecute it with all earnestness. Need I remind you that a whole ocean of actual events, of enemy success and of our own failure, does not necessarily contain for us as Christians a single drop of truth? The recognition that we under-estimated others and over-estimated ourselves is a good and necessary thing. This recognition, however, has nothing to teach us about what is right or wrong or about the responsibility and decision which follow on our knowledge of right or wrong. I cannot think that your judgment of to-day about the fundamental situation between Hitler and the rest of us is different from a year ago just because in the meantime Hitler has had so many good days (vividly reminding us of Job xxi and Psalms x and lxxiii) and France, together with all those other countries, so many bad days. If that were your attitude, you would have surrendered, not merely to the German arms, but to that German philosophy which in 1933 broke out like a plague among the German people themselves. In that case, Hitler would have conquered not only your country but your souls. I not only hope, but I know, that this is not so—in any case not so far as you, the sons and heirs of the French Reformation, are concerned. I know you are still able and willing to see through the terrible fog of a confusion between the Word of God and the language of brutal facts, just as in Germany itself I know people who have shown to this day the capacity and will to see through this confusion. I take it for granted that among your Roman Catholic brethren too, and also among the true heirs of the Revolution of 1789, there are not lacking those who have refused to be seduced by the false lure of the German realism of 1933. But to you, at least, the sharers of my own faith, I can press home the proposition that in regard to the grounds, the necessity and the right of the war against Hitler—even though it is at the moment not your war, but is being waged by others in the Channel, over London, in Egypt (and who knows where to-morrow?)— for you too nothing has changed, nothing at all. National Socialism itself, with its lies and cruelties, its arbitrary justice, its persecution of the Jews and concentration camps, its attacks upon, and poisoning of, the Christian Church, its fundamental denial of freedom and consequently of responsibility for thought and speech, its conscious and wicked repudiation of spiritual values—National Socialism as " the Revolution of Nihilism ", has not changed, even in the smallest particular. It has only proved itself to be more efficient in war than we thought and become more powerful than we wished. It has only conquered a certain number of nations, including your own, just as it first conquered the German nation, the most unfortunate of all. It has merely won a further opportunity of applying its methods in Poland, Norway and Holland, and it seems probable that France too will quickly have the chance, if it has not had it already, of learning what they are.

Do you know what it is that at the present time exercises the minds of Christians in Germany belonging to the Confessional Church more than the whole war? It is the putting to death on medical grounds, of certain " incurably " sick persons, carried out as a system on a large scale and made immune from criticism by the power of the police. Rumour has it that up to the present there have been 80,000 victims of this system. This is Hitler. To withstand this Hitler, when after mastering his own people he began to hurl himself against other nations and countries, was the clear purpose with which England and France in the autumn of 1939, after long hesitation, entered into the war. The fact that since then things have gone so extraordinarily well for Hitler and so badly for his opponents, that he has found in Europe and Asia allies among those who by their own nature were bound sooner or later to become such, that to-day he exalts himself like a god to force a new order of his own making upon the whole world, all this is no reason whatever for abandoning that purpose. For you also, even though you are at present no longer actually at war, all this is no reason for being untrue to that purpose. You must at least in your inmost heart be with those Frenchmen who have decided, and who have the opportunity of giving effect to the decision, to continue to carry on the war of the France of 1939. National Socialism is the same terrible, but at the same time inwardly empty and in the last resort utterly unreal, product of the underworld that it always has been. " One word shall quickly slay it," is as true to-day as yesterday. You, dear friends, can in fact remain neutral in this conflict no more to-day than yesterday.

If I have been well informed and understand the matter rightly, there is much talk in Christian circles in the France of to-day about the humility with which one ought to acknowledge and accept the " total defeat " as a divine judgment. And further, about the penitence which is now necessary. And again, about a sorrowful silence in which one must address oneself to the modest tasks which still remain, or are beginning to emerge, under the provisional arrangements of the armistice. Much talk also about prayer, about preaching Christ crucified, about creating, preserving and encouraging a new public spirit, as the only possible way for you to co-operate to-day in matters which are the common concern of the Christian Church and the legal State. I understand all this, and I am doing my best to understand it with sympathy and trust. For I am a little disturbed by the fact that I seem to have heard all this before; that is to say, in the Germany after 1933, when she was overrun by National Socialism. At that time and in Germany it implied a retreat of Christianity from responsibility in ecclesiastical and political spheres to the inner sphere of a religious attitude which, in order to maintain itself, no longer concerned itself with, or at least was not willing to fight and suffer for, the right form of the Church, let alone that of the State. At that time and in Germany, all this meant the sanctioning of National Socialism by a rightly or, it may be, wrongly interpreted Lutheranism. Be perfectly clear that the demonic power of National Socialism of which you have now had experience yourselves, at any rate passively, is connected with the fact that

Christianity in Germany did thus retreat. By recalling what took place in the Church struggle in Germany I certainly do not mean to say that those who to-day in France use the language of which I have spoken are already involved in this retreat. I only want to say that the promulgation of these sentiments, however well intentioned and relatively justified in the beginning, might be the first step in such a retreat, in which the Church would play directly into the hands of the arch-enemy and, in any case, of National Socialism. You will see to it that this does not happen.

Humility is an excellent thing. There is certainly no occasion for pride and, if we have been proud in the past, we have during the last half-year suffered a rude blow in the face. I am, however, troubled about the relation of this sudden emphasis on penitence both to the policy of the Vichy Government and to the apathy into which, if I am rightly informed, the great mass of your people has now sunk in the face of these fateful events. Is it not almost too much of an accommodation to the spirit of the times to fasten on humility as the preacher's theme to-day? But let that be as it may. Let us only be sure that, if we preach about humility, it is a humility before God of which we are speaking, and not a humility before facts and circumstances, before Powers and Dominions, before men and human authorities. Humility before God can have nothing to do with resignation, nor with a stunned petrifaction before a destiny which we must recognize, at any rate for the time being, to be in a certain sense unalterable. If we were to give way to this, we should have surrendered our faith and the enemy would already have triumphed over us. The secret of Hitler's being is that he knows how to produce this petrifaction all around him. Any true Christian preaching of humility in France to-day must keep far away from this kind of stupefaction.

It follows, if we are thinking of humility before God, that there can be no talk of " *total defeat* ". Has not the idea too many painful associations with the " total " purposes and claims of our adversary? How have we Christians come to apply the word " total " to anything but God's omnipotent grace? When and how can a human defeat become " total ", unless Christians involved in it were to lose their faith in the omnipotent grace of God, and with it their inward joy and the courage to bear their Christian witness? It is this that must never be allowed to happen.

It follows, if we are thinking of humility before God, that the acknowledgment and acceptance of *God's judgment* will certainly not mean that we shall grow weary and allow ourselves to become confused about what we previously recognized to be God's commandment and will, and tried to carry out in obedience to Him. God's judgment is directed not against our obedience, but against the endless disobedience with which we have again and again overlaid our little bit of obedience. If God has judged us, He has been gracious to us; He has not in judging us cast us out into a self-chosen neutrality, but given us a new beginning and encouraged us to a purer obedience.

It follows that the *repentance* which is needed will not be limited to an unfruitful, merely general, submissiveness or a passive regret for faults committed in the past; still less will it find expression in forms of renewal and innovation which will in fact help the old Adam to even greater triumphs. But true repentance (in regard, for example, to liberty, equality and fraternity) will make us wholly in earnest where formerly we were light-minded, joyful where we were sceptical, strong where we were weak and slack. Repentance will lead us to watch and not to sleep; it will guide our steps to life and not to death.

It follows that *silence*, which has certainly much to commend it, will not be a mournful silence, but the natural and fruitful self-restraint of those who have privately too much to do to indulge freely in talk.

It follows that *prayer* will not lead us away from political thought and action of a modest but definite kind, but will rather lead us directly into purposeful conflict.

It follows that the new *public spirit* will be not only a goal, not only the subject of all kinds of teaching, pastoral work, and discussion, but, above all and at once, a beginning— the spirit of a Christian repudiation of defeat, the spirit of a Christian approach to a new and better resistance, the spirit of the Christian hope which is not disposed to leave the field to the demons. How in the world can this spirit be created, maintained and encouraged except by practising it?

More than ever, and perhaps nowhere so much as in the France of to-day will the *crucified Christ*, if we are thinking of humility before God, be preached as the *risen Christ*— as the King, whose Kingdom has no boundaries, and whose servants can have no fear because He has overcome the world.

If I could understand them in this way, and could correct them a little, I should agree with these emphases. They would *not* mean that the *Church* of France has concluded an armistice. It is just this that the Church cannot and must not do, neither in the terms we have been considering nor in any others. In the Church in France the spiritual war must still go on. She cannot on any terms conclude a peace, or even an armistice, with Hitler. And in the Church in France, it must be, and remain, perfectly clear that even the military armistice which the Vichy Government made with Hitler, can have only a provisional character.

Here I want to break off, though I know that it is just here that the practical questions begin. I lack the competence to take part in the discussion of these questions. Above all, the question of " Vichy "! You may imagine that I have my own opinion about it, and also an idea what my attitude would be were I a Frenchman. But I am not a Frenchman, and I consider it better in this matter, which is your special concern, to say only what I must say explicitly—that precisely in this matter your attitude is of decisive importance in the answering of my question and the fulfilment of my request.

I commend you, dear friends and brethren, to our God in all the difficult, temptation-strewn, dangerous ways which lie before you. May His peace, which passes all understanding, keep your hearts and minds, and the hearts and minds of us all, in Christ Jesus.

With brotherly greetings!

KARL BARTH.

Basle, October 1940.

III

BooKS BY PROFESSOR BARTH THAT HAVE BEEN TRANSLATED INTO ENGLISH.

Christian Life (S.C.M. Press, 1930).
The Epistle to the Romans (O.U.P., 1933).
The Resurrection of the Dead (Hodder & Stoughton, 1933).
Theological Existence To-day (Hodder & Stoughton, 1933).
**Come, Holy Spirit* (T. and T. Clark, 1934).
**God's Search for Man* (T. and T. Clark, 1935).
The Word of God and the Word of Man (Hodder & Stoughton, 1935).
God in Action (T. and T. Clark, 1936).
Credo (Hodder and Stoughton, 1936).
The Doctrine of the Word of God (T. and T. Clark, 1936).
The Church and the Churches (J. Clarke, 1937).
The Holy Ghost and the Christian Life (Muller, 1938).
The Knowledge of God and the Service of God (Hodder & Stoughton, 1938).
Trouble and Promise in the Struggle of the Church in Germany (O.U.P., 1938).
Church and State (S.C.M. Press, 1939).
The Church and the Political Problem of Our Day (Hodder & Stoughton, 1939).

* In collaboration with E. Thurneysen.

Made in the USA
Monee, IL
07 July 2026

56551510R00036